Dedicated to all Educators
THANK YOU FOR EDUCATING

Political Advertising Manual
ISBN-13: 9780983594642 (PRINT)
ISBN-13: 978-0-9835946-8-0 (EBOOK)
Copyright© 2011 by Mikazuki Publishing House
Author: Kambiz Mostofizadeh
Illustrations by: Hoornaz Mostofizadeh & Public domain images were used.
Library of Congress Control Number: 2012900392
Publisher: Mikazuki Publishing House
www.MikazukiPublishingHouse.com
Except for use in a review, the reproduction or utilization of this work in any form or by an electronic, mechanical, or other means, now known or hereafter invented, including xerography, photocopying, recording, in any information storage and retrieval system, is forbidden and prohibited without the written permission of the author.

WARNING: DO NOT ATTEMPT ANY TECHNIQUES YOU SEE IN THIS BOOK UNLESS UNDER THE SUPERVISION OF A PROFESSIONAL POLITICAL CONSULTANT.

DISCLAIMER: THE PUBLISHER AND AUTHOR ACCEPT NO RESPONSIBILITY FOR YOUR ACTIONS BASED ON THIS BOOK.

The information contained within this book is for educational and commercial purposes and does not necessarily reflect the views of the publisher.

CONTENTS

Introduction 3
Political Science Basics 5
Advertising Marries Politics! 7
The Political Marketing Mix 8
Creating an Organization 10
Shaping Your Message 12
Opposition Research 15
Creating Effective Direct Mail Pieces 17
Bulk Email Marketing 21
Sign this Petition 23
Lawnsign Wars 25
Websites with the Wow Factor 30
Television Ads Work! 34
The Press Release Beast 42
Fall For My Robocall 46
Event Appearances 49
Phone Banking Paradise 51
T-Shirts for All 55
Canvassing 58
Townhall Meetings 60
Editorial Mastery 61
Controlling the Internet Mind Share 63
Labor Organizing & Alliances 65
Organizing a Rally or Protest 70
Creating a Political Action Committee 78
Get out the Vote 80
Political Report Card – You Flunk! 82
Political Advertising Glossary 84
Political Art 97
Why Politics is Vital 99
Bibliography 100
Notes 101
Acknowledgments 110

INTRODUCTION

I graduated with honors with a Bachelor Degree in Political Science from California State University of Dominguez Hills. I had the honor of learning from many great professors that I have recognized in the acknowledgment section of this book. During my period of education at CSU Dominguez Hills, I had the pain of experiencing hundreds of millions of dollars being cut per year from California's higher education budget. I felt that getting involved was not only an important step to saving education, but more so an opportunity for me to express my frustration with the denial of funds to higher education resulting in the denial of resources needed to educate tomorrow's leaders. I used the techniques I have expressed in this book to organize 6 protests and rallies to stop academic budget cuts, work on eight political campaigns, and run for Los

Angeles City Council in 2011. I thought that sharing my knowledge and experience would empower individuals to use political advertising for advancing the greater good. In this book, when I refer to advertising, I am referring to message delivery. When I refer to politics, I am referring to the root demands that a group or individual has in relation to an issue or cause. Advertising is the method by which the politics creates results.

MOSTOFIZADEH'S HIERARCHY OF POLITICS

POLITICAL SCIENCE BASICS

Major Legislative Powers of the Congress

The major powers of the United States Congress are to tax, appropriate, regulate commerce, establish courts with jurisdictions, declare war, approve treaties, approve appointments such as Ambassadorships, propose amendments to the Constitution, impeach officials, discipline a Congressmember, or do anything that is necessary for maintaining its operations.

The House of Representatives has 435 seats that are apportioned to the states by their population and are reapportioned every 10 years after the census. States are responsible for redistricting or redrawing their district lines. Elections are held every 2 years by voters in their district with the conditions that each candidate must be at least 25 years of age, a US Citizen for at least years 7 years, and a resident of the state.

The United States Senate has 100 seats with every state having 2 seats each. Elections are held every 6 years with 1/3 of the seats up for election every 2 years. Therefore only 1/3 of the seats are up for election every 2 years. The conditions for running for US Senate are that the candidate must be at least 30 years of age, a US Citizen for at least 9 years, and a resident of the state he/she wishes to represent.

With over 50,000 elections being held over the course of every 7 years in the United States, there are many positions that have to be filled. The question is, will you fill them or will they be filled by individuals less qualified, less educated, and less experienced than you?

ADVERTISING MARRIES POLITICS

There are no exact dates as to when the first unification or marriage of advertising and politics occurred. Stanley Kelley is widely recognized as the first person to have used the term "political marketing." There are some that believe it started thousands of years ago, when the first leader spoke to his supporters, delivering a speech about an issue. The ability to make noise or deliver a message is what gave the individual the power to draw in followers. Without the use of message delivery, no leader would be able to attract supporters.

Advertising and marketing are used interchangeably by media reporters and writers. Advertising is the physical creation and distribution of your message. Marketing is the overall field in which advertising is a part. In politics there are many fields and sub-fields however, political marketing uses the field of the study of campaigns and elections from political science and incorporates this with the creation and distribution of the message.

THE POLITICAL MARKETING MIX

The famous 4 P's of marketing created by Professor Edmund McCarthy are Product, Promotion, Price, and Place. The 3 P's of political marketing are Political Issue, Political Branding, and Political Cost.

ISSUE

The product in political marketing is the issue or the candidate. A clear presentation must be made extolling the reasons not only the experience, but more importantly the vision. Issues are able to influence individuals to change parties and influence their other views as well. For example, an individual that uses the term "gun control" would more likely tend to vote or support Democratic or liberal issues. An individual that uses the term "pro-life" would more likely tend to vote or support Republican issues. The stance or viewpoints that individuals take on certain issues will more likely than not determine how they will view other issues.

BRANDING

A candidate or issue that is not seen by the public, will not receive support or donations from the public.. It is vital to use press releases, social network marketing, media interviews, speeches, canvassing, and targeted advertisements to generate awareness in regards to your issue or candidate. The attitude that should be maintained is that of striving to keep the issue in the public agenda.

POLITICAL COST

The first thing a potential supporter asks of themselves is "why should I support this person or organization." Supporters do not want to support a candidate or an issue that have little or no chances of advancing or winning. No one likes to join the losing team. The more money that political campaigns are able to raise in the early stages of the campaign, the greater the chances of success.

CREATING AN ORGANIZATON

The success of your political campaign, whether issue based or candidate based, will depend on your ability to create an organization that executes effectively.

Campaign Manager: Responsible for managing and overseeing the overall campaign.

Political Director: Responsible for planning, creating

strategies based on information from campaign officers.

Volunteer Coordinator: Campaign officer responsible for recruiting individuals to carry out various tasks during the campaign including phone banking, canvassing, and other related tasks.

Community Relations Director: Campaign officer responsible for establishing relationships with unions, associations, groups, clubs, and other organizations for the purpose of achieving their support.

Scheduler: Campaign officer responsible for maintaining the campaign's official calendar of events and notifying the relevant parties.

Opposition Research Director: Conducts a thorough investigation and analysis in regards to the opponents, competitors, and supporters of the campaign.

SHAPING YOUR MESSAGE

Creating a message that resonates with your target audience depends on the use of polls and surveys to better gauge the importance of various issues to potential voters or supporters. The ability to communicate is not the ability to politically communicate. An important study by Valentino, Hutchins, and Williams, published by the International Communication Association, stated that political advertising effects those most who have an understanding of the complex range of issues that define politics. **(2)**

In advertising major products, many Fortune 500 companies depend on the slick productions of ad agencies that have been better suited selling soap and laundry detergent. The messages in many political advertising campaigns are vague and it is many times difficult for the reader to decode what the message is that is being conveyed. In politics, a message must contain two important elements:

- **ISSUE** – People support issues and it is their support of these issue that guide their decision making process when supporting a candidate, cause, organization, or party.
- **VISION** – This is where you provide a solution that will solve the problem or the issue that exists. The vision is what you plan on doing to fix the issue and how the stakeholders(public, supporters, voters, people affected by the issue, etc.) affected by the issue) can participate.

STRATEGIES TO REMEMBER

Win Big, Lose Big – It is better to focus on areas that you will win and politically abandon areas you will lose. To attempt to win in an area that you will most likely lose big in is not only a waste of resources, but also will tire your volunteers.

Mimicking the opponent – This strategy attempts to present your political positions in a manner that nearly copies the opponent, with the added bonus of variations that will create value.

Negative Focused – This strategy attempts to destroy the credibility of an issue, a political candidate, or opponent. This strategy cannot win campaigns, but it can be used with effectiveness to ruin an opponent's campaign or to pressure a politician or organization to a specific political stance.

Populist – This strategy takes into consideration the common peoples issues over that of the status quo.

Flanking – This strategy attempts to "monopolize" political positions left undefended or shunned by opponents.

OPPOSITION RESEARCH

If you want to execute an effective campaign that delivers a message that resonates with voters, first you must understand what your competitors are saying. Your strategy and your message should be crafted based on the positioning of your opponents. If you are not facing competitors and are facing opponents or individuals that are working against your issue, it is important to identify who they are. A spreadsheet should be created with the following fields; name, address , phone number ,email, aliases, civil lawsuits, penal crimes, lawsuits, injunctions, liens, and other important information you can gather. The most important information you should be seeking is politically damaging information including fines by a governmental ethics commission and damaging comments quoted in news sources. The best information is that can be used against the candidate, organization, or opposition at a later time.

As a general rule of a political campaign, opposition research is the first step undertaken from which information is gathered to plan the campaign strategy. There are professional firms that specialize in opposition research that you can outsource this vital task to. If your campaign has access to limited resources, an internet connection and a laptop will suffice. Search the major search engine service providers using Boolean search methods for greater results. Every individual has left a trail in one form or another from which ample information could be harvested from. After the campaign strategy has been created from the information on the opponents, the political atmosphere in which the operations are occurring have weighed and resources have been made available for expending, does the political advertising begins.

CREATING EFFECTIVE DIRECT MAIL

Direct mail is a powerful tool for any political advertising campaign and it should be used frequently to garner support and donations. Writing an effective direct mail piece that motivates supporters to take action depends on the following:

IMPORTANCE & RELEVANCE OF THE ISSUE

Although the candidate or issue is important to you, that does not necessarily mean that people will have the same feelings that you do. An issue such as homelessness will have a larger amount of potential supporters than will saving the pacific ocean wolf eel. If you are unable to gain supporters because your issue lacks the "critical mass" needed for gaining supporters, you will be facing a difficult battle that you may not be able to win.

THE FORMAT OF THE LETTER

The direct mail piece should be written by a professional or someone that has had prior experience drafting such letters.

The direct mail letter has 5 parts:

Introduction

Dear (NAME OF RECIPIENT),

My name is **(YOUR NAME)** and I'm asking you to support **(NAME OF CANDIDATE OR ISSUE OR ORGANIZATION)**. We have countless years of experience in increasing college retention rates, creating jobs, and boosting union participation.

Problem

(We/Name of Candidate/Name of Organization) are determined to stop the academic budget cuts made to teachers and students. Over a billion dollars has been cut from the academic budget for education resulting in cancelled classes and a lower quality of education. Year after year we have heard excuses and have not seen any change. Career politicians have rushed to point their fingers at the declining support for public education while they have laid back, collected a pay check and allowed our education to suffer.

Solution

We are building local neighborhood action centers to garner support for public education and we need your help. We wish to build **(QUANTITY OR UNITS)** neighborhood centers across **(the name of the area)**.

Call to Action

Right now you have the opportunity to do something that is never been done in **(NAME OF CITY/NAME OF DISTRICT/NAME OF AREA)**, and that is to tell career politicians that you are tired of their excuses and you won't take it any longer.

We are asking you to **(DONATE/WRITE A LETTER TO/VOTE FOR/SUPPORT) (ISSUE/CANDIDATE/NAME OF ORGANIZATION/CAUSE)**. With your support, we can have the necessary tool to solve the problems in **(NAME OF ISSUE/NAME OF GEOGRAPHICAL AREA)**.

We sincerely hope that we can count on your support.

Name of Authority

Sincerely,

(SIGNATURE)

(YOUR NAME/NAME OF ENDORSER/NAME OF PUBLIC FIGURE)
(COMMITTEE NAME/ORGANIZATION NAME)
(YOUR PHONE NUMBER)
(EMAIL ADDRESS)
(WEBSITE ADDRESS)

SAMPLE DIRECT MAIL LETTER

(YOUR COMMITTEE NAME)
CAMPAIGN HEADQUARTERS

Dear **(NAME OF RECIPIENT)**,

My name is **(YOUR NAME)** and I'm asking you to support (NAME OF CANDIDATE OR ISSUE OR ORGANIZATION). We have countless years of experience in increasing college retention rates, creating jobs, and boosting union participation.

(We/Name of Candidate/Name of Organization) are determined to stop the academic budget cuts made to teachers and students. Over a billion dollars has been cut from the academic budget for education resulting in cancelled classes and a lower quality of education. Year after year we have heard excuses and have not seen any change.

Career politicians have rushed to point their fingers at the declining support for public education while they have laid back, collected a pay check and allowed our education to suffer. We are building local neighborhood action centers to garner support for public education and we need your help.

We wish to build (QUANTITY OR UNITS) neighborhood centers across (the name of the area). Right now you have the opportunity to do something that is never been done in (NAME OF CITY/NAME OF DISTRICT/NAME OF AREA), and that is to tell career politicians that you are tired of their excuses and you won't take it any longer.

We are asking you to (DONATE/WRITE A LETTER TO/VOTE FOR/SUPPORT) (ISSUE/CANDIDATE/NAME OF ORGANIZATION/CAUSE). With your support, we can have the necessary tool to solve the problems in (NAME OF ISSUE/NAME OF GEOGRAPHICAL AREA).
We sincerely hope that we can count on your support.

Sincerely,

(SIGNATURE)

(YOUR NAME/NAME OF ENDORSER/NAME OF PUBLIC FIGURE)
(COMMITTEE NAME/ORGANIZATION NAME)
(YOUR PHONE NUMBER)
(EMAIL ADDRESS)
(WEBSITE ADDRESS)

BULK EMAIL MARKETING

Email political marketing can be used with effectiveness to notify and deliver your political message to thousands of individuals simultaneously. Bulk email or electronic mail sent by the hundreds or thousands should be executed using a professional bulk email delivery provider such as ConstantContact or MailChimp. The anatomy of the email sent, the lists used to send the correspondence, and the system used for delivering the emails, assist in the probability of an individual opening the email. First, the subject of the email should be relevant, eye-catching, and attractive. Use a graphic template for your email to make your message more appealing. You can create a graphic template from scratch or edit one that is provided by the bulk email service provider you are using. Secondly, in the body of the email, create a message that clearly conveys the political platform of the campaign, how the individuals receiving the email are affected by the issues, and a call to action so that supporters can take a political action. Thirdly, check the entire email for brand continuity to ensure the colors, logo, graphics, and message are the same as the rest of the marketing materials being used in the campaign.

SIGN THIS PETITION

The process of being able to solicit individuals to sign a petition to qualify for political office or to create a referendum based on a political initiative, is the essence of the democratic process. Gathering signature en masse', depends on the existence and coordination of several factors to achieve success.

ELEMENTS

- Blank petitions with clipboards and pens
- Trained signature gatherers

Before signature gatherers start soliciting individuals to sign the petitions, they must be thoroughly trained in the petition forms being used so as to prevent mistakes that could nullify your efforts. On average, you have to take into consideration that up to 35% of the signatures you gather, may not be verifiable. That is the reason why it is essential to gather 135% of the signatures required, rather than 100%.

POINTS OF PETITION (POP)

Points of Petition (POP) are areas you're your signature gatherers come face to face with a potential petition signer. Permission should be sought in most cases as a rule, to prevent violations of the law.

Community Colleges & Universities – Places of higher education are excellent locations because you potentially have access to tens of thousands of registered voters.

Major Shopping Centers – Places with many shops tend to draw in thousands of people per day giving you access to many registered voters.

Homes of Registered Voters – The residents of registered voters will yield the highest amount of signatures for your campaign.

LAWN SIGN WARS

Lawnsigns are 12x18 or 18x24 inch signs placed in front of homes, in windows of businesses, on street poles, and in other public areas so as to promote maximum visibility. Lawnsigns cost between one to two dollars per piece and are an effective way to promote the message of the political advertising campaign in as many places as possible. It is easy to source lawn signs for one to two dollars per piece and no campaign should be paying more than this amount. The distribution of lawn signs occur to homes and businesses. Businesses, being high traffic, are excellent locations for posting a lawn sign in. The initial creation of the relationship by a representative of the campaign is vital for the successful implementation of the method. The representative responsible for the distribution of the lawn signs should focus on street that have a high flow of traffic, thereby targeting stores that can be approached for posting the signs. Representatives seeking stores should not be too selective, so as to the limit the amount of stores that can be approached. All stores on high traffic streets are potential targets for approach, and storeowners will view the sign as a tool for gaining new business. **(1)**

Between three hundred to one thousand signs should be used, depending on the size of the area you are operating in. Double sided allow greater exposure than one sided signs, but they are more expensive. Depending on the placement areas available, you will have to decide whether the costs of using double sided signs are greater than the benefits.

Installation of the signs requires two persons, a step ladder, and zip ties to hold the signs in place. If you are installing the signs on fences or in the ground, the stake or stakes attached to each sign will be sufficient to hold the sign in place. Many candidate and issue based campaigns make the mistake of confusing message delivery using signs, with a sign war. More signs doesn't equate to greater support for your candidate or issue if the signs are placed in an area that is opposed to your candidate or issue. Signs placed in locations that disrupt scenery or cause an obstruction, could create a negative backlash for the candidate or issue.

Lawnsign locations can also be sought using phone banking to ask potential location owners to allow their property to host a lawnsign. An individual experienced with phone banking, political issues, and answering questions related to the campaign, should be responsible for contacting the location owners.

Heavily trafficked streets are perfect locations for placement and every effort should be made to secure these locations first. The caller(s) should use a standard script without deviation in order to reach the intended results.

SAMPLE SCRIPT

Hi. My name is (your name).

I am calling from (Campaign Name/Committee Name).

Can I speak to the owner or resident?
We are calling you because we need your help.

There have been deep cuts recently in the academic budgets that provide public education. We are asking for your support by allowing us to place a lawnsign at your location.

Can we count on your support?

    a. **IF NO** – We understand. Please visit www.YOURDOMAIN.com and please do not hesitate to contact us in the future. Thank you for considering us. Have a nice day. Goodbye.

b. **IF YES** - Thank you for supporting us. We will be in the area next week, and will be placing lawnsigns in the nearby area. With your permission, we will place the lawnsign on your location. We would like to thank you for the support and look forward to speak with you soon. Please call (Your phone number) if you have any problems with the sign or questions. Thank you and have a nice day. Goodbye.

WEBSITES WITH THE WOW FACTOR

Creating a website for your candidate or issue based campaign that properly conveys your message, explains why they should get involved, gives them ways to get involved, and gives them ways to stay involved.

The website for your issue or campaign will have a:

Home Page

The home page is the entry point, first impression, & way to the rest of the site. The home page should feature a key art image. The key art image is an image that you will be throughout the campaign so as to mentally reinforce the image with the name of the candidate or issue. The use of a countdown timer is beneficial because it will create a sense of urgency for the viewer. The home page should also feature information regarding the platform or theme of the campaign. The buttons on the home page should feature About Us or Biography, Endorsements, Issues, Media, Donate Now, and Contact Us.

About Us (Issue) or Biography (Candidate)

The About Us or Biography page gives a

background summary of the issue or candidate to the reader. This is vital because it gives the reader a frame of reference that allows them to categorize the issue or candidate in their mind.

Endorsements

The Endorsement page features a list of all the groups, organizations, public officials, community leaders, and notable individuals that support you. This list is important for creating the perception that you have many supporters. This page should also include a form that allows the viewer to also become an endorser/supporter.

Issues

The Issues page gives the reader insight into the reason why you are engaging in political activity, to influence issues. Whether a candidate or issue based campaign, it is the issue(s) that define the campaign. The Issues page should give a thorough yet concise explanation of the platform or message of the campaign.

Media

The Media page is designed to allow newspaper reporters and journalists access to pictures, press clippings, video footage and articles related to the candidate or issue. This page ties together all the important media that the press needs for constructing an original article about the candidate or issue.

Donate Now

The Donate Now page allows the reader to take action and to support their belief in the issue by allowing them to donate. By donating, they feel they are a part of the campaign, and this gives them satisfaction. On the Donate Now page, there should be a summarization of the reasons why the reader should support the candidate or issue and how the money will be used yet concise explanation of the platform or message of the campaign.

Contact Us

The Contact Us page should feature a form to make contacting you more user friendly and should have your email , telephone number, and address listed. The design of the Contact Us page should be simple, with the focus that of conveying as many mediums of contact, (phone, email, etc.) so that your political advertising campaign can be reached without delay.

TELEVISON ADS WORK!

Televisions ads have the advantage of being able to reach tens of thousands of people simultaneously with a lower cost per viewer than radio and print. Television ads range from approximately

$7 per 30 second spot during early morning and late night to $50 per 30 second spot during primetime.

The use of emotional exchange or deliberate use of symbolism to invoke feelings and specific emotions including strength, fear, and tranquility is a key component of television advertising. The creation and production of political television advertising started with the first Checkers television ads featuring President Nixon. The four phases of political television advertising campaigns are introduced which include branding, stating your platform, attack ads, and supplying vision. According to Bruce Barton "candidates need to be humanized". The theme of change is not a new development initiated by the 2008 Obama Presidential campaign. The theme of change with the slogan "time for a change" which was used by the Republican Party in 1952 to gain power after 20 years of Democratic Rule. Madison Avenue or the advertising agencies which controlled the paid media and in some instances free media were for the most part Republican strongholds. In many cases, the Democratic Party could not find agency representation because the aforementioned ad agencies refused to assist or take on Democratic campaigns. The first television broadcasts involving political matters involved the hiring of media specialists by political parties to use techniques that had been previously successful for selling commercial goods to be able to package and sell to voters, the candidate. Political candidates were coached, prepared, trained, and taught how to present and act while on camera. Besides negative remarks regarding televised political advertising which include "celluloid image", the use of television advertising proved its success in educating voters through paid media in ways that free media was unable to do. The first televised political broadcasts were slots of air time which were purchased in 10, 30, 60 minutes block for a candidate to deliver their platform. Due to the long nature and the seriousness of political discourse, audiences grew impatient and switched channels. The use of "spots" or 30 second time blocks for delivering a political advertisement eventually went on to replace political speeches. Further techniques were then developed that would shorten the time of political message delivery and keep voters watching. The beginnings of political television advertising witnessed the creation and use of a technique known as the "blunt truth technique" which featured a man standing behind a podium facing voters and speaking.

The use of political television advertising was cemented by 1960, when nine out of ten homes had a television set. John F. Kennedy used a technique called "candidate as interviewer" successfully for a television ad which featured Kennedy interviewing farmers about their loss in wages. This style of spontaneous filming is called "cinema-verite" and was mimicked multiple times by many political campaigns. According to William Bernbach, the goal of televised political advertising is to locate the "unchanging man" or the compulsions and instincts that drive impulses and dominate our every action. The ultimate goal was the overlying strategy of appealing to the "core of being" or those various emotions which makeup our existence. The "core of being" approach used bold headlines, taut layouts, short copy, humor, and an appeal to humanity. By 1971, greater participation of African-Americans, Latinos, and other minorities in advertising agencies signaled an ideological shift in the labor pools and professional cadres of the political advertising industry. In swift contrast to 1960, a Nixon aide wrote in 1971 about the difficulty of finding conservative copywriters.

    There also began a marketing shift in televised political advertising from presenting a candidate's unique selling proposition or the candidate's distinctly identifiable differentiating quality to appealing to emotion. Nixon's successful of close-ups in television ads created intimacy between himself and audiences. Nixon was the first political candidate to pioneer the use of "targeting" or only delivering televised ads to audiences which were previously marked to receive the ads. Targeting of televised ads substantially increased advertising return on investment for candidates and enabled candidates to conserve resources by denying the delivery of televised ads which did not reach the intended viewers. In 1976, Gerald Ford's Presidential campaign versus Carter witnessed the peak of the successful use of songs in political television ads with the execution of Ford's "Feeling Good" ad campaign. The "Feeling Good" campaign had one explicit goal, to make voters feel good about the state of the union and themselves causing them to elect Gerald Ford to the Presidency. A negative impact of political television ads are the feeling of "dissonance" between the candidate as he or she is perceived by the audience viewing a television ad and the "real candidate" who is revealed through debates and speeches. This is referred to as the "Ottinger Effect". The projection of the voters desires for a candidate as an object to be the "ideal" and "model politician" often creates a scenario where the candidate is different than those ideals we project unto them.

Political television advertising is an essential tool for simultaneously reaching large amounts of voters, educating the voting population, and creating enough name recognition to generate donations. Despite negative connotations which have been attached to television advertising, it must be recognized that free media including print and online does not always give the viewer a "complete" truth. Paid media which is inherently biased nevertheless gives a version of the "truth" which the creator and/or producer of the ad seeks to project and in this manner is not extremely opposed to free media. Currently free media is viewed by paid media advertisers as a boon to companies providing them with publicity without having to expend resources. The use of paid media legitimizes political candidates and provides them with immediate prestige which tends to attract political donors. The lack of educating or creating awareness of issues among voters has been viewed as a driver of low voter turnouts and low participation in the political process. Without television advertising, viewers would not know where to seek information regarding the candidates except candidates websites which is not the ideal location for conveying political platforms. The nature of television advertising campaigns dictate the four step approach of branding the candidate or issue, presenting the candidate or issue's platform, attacking the opponent, and selling voters' on the candidate/issue's vision. Television advertising is essential and will continue to remain vital for candidates and issues to create name recognition, convey vision, present platforms, enable fundraisers, organize, recruit volunteers, and gain prestige.

THE PRESS RELEASE BEAST

The most powerful weapon in the political marketing arsenal of the candidate or issue based campaign is the press release. It is also one of the first used political advertising tools for reaching a mass audience. Since the first newspaper Acta Diurna by the Romans in the 1st Century C.E., political events have been publicized through the use of printed material to disseminate political messages. A press release is an article that is written with the intention of generating publicity for your message. Newspapers and media sources depend on the incoming flow of news because this reduces their costs of having to gather the news. Newspapers and media sources also generate more ad space, the more news they receive. The ad space fills the news and the news is used to create ad space for selling to advertisers. A press release uses the inverted pyramid formula for stimulating the reader and providing the message in a manner that shapes the perception of the reader. A standard press release is between 150-300 words, and includes the contact information of the sender. After creating the press release, the press release is edited for grammatical mistakes, and submitted to newspaper and media publication news desks. News desks are a central location in newspapers and media publications that press releases are sent to and then disseminated based on category to the relevant reporters. If the press release is being sent in relation to an event, the press release should include specific information about the event, 2-3 weeks in advance of the event, so that the reporter will have time to plan for covering the event.

SAMPLE PRESS RELEASE

(SUBJECT TITLE) New Candidate, New Vision

(BODY) Jeffrey Maloney, an education activist that graduated with Honors with a Bachelor of Arts degree in Political Science from California State University of Dominguez Hills, has officially announced his candidacy for the California Assembly. Maloney is running on a platform of (ENTER YOUR PLATFORM OR CAMPAIGN MESSAGE HERE).

NAME OF SPOKESPERSON/CANDIDATE said "California has a budget deficit that is hundreds of millions of dollars. I want to bring public accountability by reducing public waste using e-government initiatives and use the money California saves to re-invest in the creation of a Free Trade Zone (FTZ) in the Port of Los Angeles for manufacturing companies that export the majority of the products they produce.

The election for the California Assembly will be held on November 28th, 2061.

(Tells the reporter this article is ready to be printed)

The inverted pyramid is the proper method to be used with the most important information first and the least important information in the press release, printed last.

Important Press Release Contacts

New York Times - national@nytimes.com

Wall Street Journal - doug.belkin@wsj.com

Roll Call - editors@rollcall.com

Washington DC Examiner - editor@dcexaminer.com

The Washington Post - national@washpost.com

Atlanta Journal Constitution - newstips@ajc.com

San Francisco Chronicle - metro@sfchronicle.com

The Seattle Times - newstips@seattletimes.com

The Boston Globe - localnews@globe.com

NOTE!
- Do not spam
- Do not send press releases that are not newsworthy
- Do follow up press release with a phone call

FALL FOR MY ROBOCALL

A robocall is an automated phone with a pre-recorded message that is mass distributed for the purpose of delivering your message. Before you make any robocalls, you need to do a few things. First you should check the laws regarding sending robocalls so you or your organization do not get fined, secondly you need a targeted list of phone numbers that are relevant to the message you are disseminating, thirdly you need to find an automated phone call service provider to send the robocalls, fourth you need to record a message to be used in the robocall, and finally you must have a phone number to take live transfers from individuals receiving the robocalls. All robocalls must give the option to the individual receiving the call to initiate a live transfer or be transferred to a live operator. It is important that this live operator be trained in the issues and message that the robocall is extolling. Robocall service providers charge between one cent to three cents per each thirty second robocall. Robocalls should not last longer than thirty seconds because the attention span of the listener is limited.

SAMPLE ROBOCALL SCRIPT
Hi. My name is (YOUR NAME), candidate for Mayor of Calico, WY.

I am calling you because on June 5th, 2012 is the election.

I believe in creating jobs, protecting education, revitalizing neighborhoods, and protecting the rights of labor.

You will be receiving more information from us in the near future.

Feel free to contact us now at www.YourName.com. www.Y-O-U-R-N-A-M-E.com

This message was paid for by: Committee to Elect Your Name for Mayor 2012

The message that is delivered should be clear and concise, using a voice that is agreeable to listen to. Voiceover specialists can be hired at a reasonable cost but should be viewed as a vital investment for

maintaining a high quality production. Every robocall

has three parts, the introduction, the issues/message,

and the call to action.

A SAMPLE ROBOCALL

PART I - INTRODUCTION
"Hi, My name is (Your Name), I am calling from

(Your Organization's Name).

PART II – ISSUES/MESSAGE

I would like to share with you (The Issue/Message).

PART III – CALL TO ACTION
We need your support. Please (Call/Write A Letter To/Email/Vote for/Attend/Reply to)(THE CONTACT INFORMATION OF THE TARGET FOR WHICH THE ACTION IS TO BEING TAKEN).

EVENT APPEARANCES

Event appearances are an important tool for accessing large amounts of people for face to face message delivery. Many events can draw tens of thousands of people, allowing your message to reach a maximum amount of individuals for a relatively small amount of money. Five individuals are ideal for covering a large event with thousands of attendees. The key is for each individual to first be trained for at least 15-30 minutes before speaking with any individual. The training session should explain the background of the candidate and issue. The training should also include the platform or main message/theme. Also the five individuals should each have 100-200 flyer or handbills that can be distributed to individuals seeking more information. The flyer or handbill should feature the platform or main message/them and a call to action. The call to action asks them to take an action that will benefit your stance in regards to the platform.

Events should be used for the contact information of as many people and organizations as possible. This information can be used can when compiling in-house direct mailing or in-house email marketing lists. The costs of appearing at an event are the transportation costs, political advertising material costs, event entry tickets costs, providing food/and or refreshments for your team, and paying your team of representatives. Events are less costly in relation other political advertising techniques however, it is efficient and gives the public access to individuals that are trained to disseminate the message and the issues.

PHONE BANKING PARADISE

Creating a phone bank and assigning volunteers list of supporters to call, is a vital and essential part of any political campaign. Before you begin, you will first need the correct items for this section of the campaign. You will need:

Phone Bank Lists – Can be acquired from an Election Clerk or from companies that specialize in the sale of voter lists. It is important that the lists you use or generate, have been updated within the past 18 months. The more targeted your lists are, the higher your chances are of achieving success. Lists can be filtered and compiled according to voter history, education level, income, age, and other key variables. For example, lets argue that individuals that have a bachelors degree or higher, tend to vote more than individuals with only a high school diploma. If this is indeed true, then it would only be logical to target voters that have a bachelors degree or higher in order to maximize your political campaign advertising dollars.

Phone Bank Volunteers – The Volunteer Coordinator is responsible for recruiting individuals to make calls. Before any phone calls are placed by the volunteers, a one hour training session should be given with relevant information and practice using the Official Phone Bank Script.

Official Phone Bank Script – This script should be written by an individual with credible experience in politics, advertising, and sales. The script should then be viewed by the Political Director and the Campaign Manager for comments and/or changes.

The purpose of creating a phone bank is in order to establish a central location for the mass distribution and reception of phone calls. If you are specifically using this phone bank to garner support for an issue, raise donations, receive affirmation of being able to place a lawnsign in a given location, or are trying to influence a voter to support a candidate for political office, then you will use the following method:

1. Make the phone call
2. Read from Official Phone Bank Script
3. Ask for the individual to support your campaign (donations, Lawnsigns, votes, etc.)

Voter Identification

The purpose of voter identification or voter ID, is to be able to know beforehand which of the eligible voters in that given area, will be voting for your candidate (YES'S), voting against your candidate (NO'S), or is not sure how they will be voting. Do not despair, because a large percentage of voters do not know who they will vote for until they are in the voting booth. Yes's are given a value of 1, No's a value of 2, and Maybe's are a 3. On a daily basis, the number of 1's, the number of 2's, and the number of 3's are tallied. If 3000 votes are required to win an election, by having near real time updates in regards to the number of 1's, is beneficial to a political campaign, when trying to reach the needed number of voters. There should a high rate of calls, that should be monitored by a campaign officer, that gives information in regards to the number of phone calls placed per hour, per person. This information can be used by the Campaign Manager, Political Director, and Volunteer Coordinator, for planning to achieve higher productivity. It is important to note that, just because you have received 3000 YES'S does not mean your candidate will win. These YES'S must be called within the 3 days before the election to remind them to vote. On GOTV day, they should be called again as a reminder. Voters that are YES'S that do not have transportation to the voting booth, should be given complimentary pickup and return to and from the voting booth if needed.

T-SHIRTS FOR ALL!

T-Shirts are an inexpensive giveaway that potential supporters will be glad to accept as a gift. They will cost you $1 to $3 per piece, depending on if you have them professionally silkscreened or if you do them yourself. If you have them professionally silkscreened, the cost per piece should be no more than $3 per piece but the product is long lasting. I recommend creating your own t-shirts if you have limited resources.

Producing T-Shirts In-House

You can purchase 8.5 x 11 inch inkjet thermal transfer paper and a iron to make t-shirts for approximately $1.50 per piece. You will need to also have a color inkjet printer, plain shirt, and a ironing table to produce your own t-shirts. There are many brick & mortar stores and online stores where you can find t-shirts being sold in bulk amounts. If you are unable to source a store near you or an online store that is satisfactory for your budget, the best places to visit are the wholesalers in the fabric and textile section in the downtown area of your city. Plain t-shirts should cost between $1 to $1.50 maximum. An inkjet printer can be sourced online for as little as $50. 8.5 x 11 inch thermal inkjet transfer paper costs as little as $.30 cents per sheet if purchase in bulk packages of 100. First you must select your image that you will use and open that file in a software package that allows you to manipulate the image. Secondly, you must "mirror" the image so that it is flipped in a manner that is readable to the human eye. If you do not do this, your t-shirt images will print out backwards and will only be read if you are facing a mirror. Thirdly, when you print the image on to the inkjet thermal transfer paper, you should allow the ink to dry so the image does not smear on the shirt when being applied. When the image on the transfer paper dries, apply the paper on to a t-shirt and iron over the image for 15 minutes. Apply even heat and pressure when ironing and put the t-shirt to the side so that it cools. Do not remove the transfer paper off of the t-shirt for 30 minutes or else the printed image on the t-shirt will be matte instead of glossy.

T-shirts should be used in multiple ways to increase exposure and branding of your issue, organization, or candidate. For maximum exposure, all of the individuals participating in the campaign should be wearing the t-shirts during signature gathering, event appearances, canvassing door-to-door, and during various campaign activities. When all individuals in the campaign are wearing the t-shirt, the image projected to potential supporters is that of professionalism.

CANVASSING

Canvassers are volunteers assigned by the Volunteer Coordinator or Political Director, to knock on the doors of registered voters with the goal of:

- Making the voters politically aware of the candidate and/or the issue(s).
- Gauging the level of support from the registered voter.
- Getting a donation, receiving a promise to vote, placing a lawnsign, and/or gaining political support.

The canvassers should be trained before **(2)** speaking with registered voters and should carry blank voter registration forms in case they canvass a home whose occupants are not registered to vote. Canvassers should apply the aforementioned formula of introducing the candidate/issue, gauging the level of support from the registered voter, and asking the registered voter to take an action to help the campaign achieve success.

Based on each canvasser spending an average of three minutes at each home, one canvasser could theoretically cover twenty homes per hour. A team of five canvassers working efficiently, could reach 500 homes in a five hour shift.

Key Canvassing Strategies

Only Registered Voters Homes – By focusing on registered voters only, you have a high chance of reaching politically active individuals.

Literature Drops – Instead of knocking on doors, your canvassers drop off campaign literature.

TOWNHALL MEETINGS

Townhall meetings are events created by the campaign organization with the purpose of selling the campaign's official views on an issue or issues. They are stage events in that the questions are prepared and are known beforehand by the individuals that will answer them. A place for the event is selected that has ample room to seat an audience of at least 30 people. A P.A. or public announcement system is used that includes a microphone connected to an amplifier with speakers. There are seats aligned in rows facing the podium from which the questions will be answered. Townhall meetings are advertised at least 4-6 weeks before the event using social network marketing, internet events, mailers sent to relevant parties, emails sent by the thousands, phone calls made, and 11x17 cardstock ads are placed on street poles. Townhall meetings are a little more costly than other forms of political advertising however, they have the ability to generate interest in the community resulting in greater attendance numbers. The costs of a Townhall meeting are political marketing materials including flyers or handbills, the cost of renting a venue for hosting the event, and refreshments for attendees. Simple refreshments should be provided; coffee and tea, donuts, and water.

EDITORIAL MASTERY

Newspapers are excellent resources for community information and are still read in one form or another. As an element of the campaign, writing editorials or letters to the editor assist in generating public awareness in regards to the issues you are politically advertising. In political marketing as in warfare, it is necessary to win the "hearts and minds" of those you are targeting. An editorial campaign within the overall campaign is a war of creating awareness for matters that are not in the public sphere. Complex political advertising is effective for those with an understanding of the complex range of issues contained within politics however, in communicating the campaign's message to an audience that is less politically savvy, it will require the insertion of your message in potential supporters' minds at a base level. No images or slick advertising productions, just pure textual arguments. The larger the number of editorial writers you have and the greater the amount of editorial articles you submit to editors of newspapers, determines your chances of having your letters printed. Lists of editorial newspaper contacts can be found in most libraries.

CONTROLLING THE INTERNET MIND SHARE

The internet is the most likely place people turn to when looking for information about politics. The mere number of choices and the ability to access locations outside the U.S. gives campaigns that are internet-centric, a competitive advantage. The widespread adoption of Facebook and Twitter have created a platform mass message dissemination with little effort. It is important to create a Facebook page and invite friends to become fans. Update the Facebook regularly and do not engage in political debates with anyone. Delete outright negative or explicit comments. You can posts videos and pictures from the campaign on the Facebook page. The Facebook page can also be used for creating events. After you create the event, invite friends and share the event on your page. The ability for a campaign to make a 5 minute video explaining the issues and then upload it to YouTube for instant viewing is vital. Between four to six videos should be created that give a background of the issues or candidate and giving a call to action. A campaign can even host a live event while broadcasting it live on UStream. Blogs should be created on WordPress, Blogger, and free blog sites. Weekly emails should be sent out using an email service provider such as ConstantContact or MailChimp with in-house and/or purchased opt-in email lists. Internet press releases can be delivered for a relatively low price using press release dissemination sites like PRWeb and PRNewswire. YouTube should be used a main location for distributing your message to a mass audience. If you are not a professional video editor, then it is common practice to hire someone to edit your video for you. If you have time available, there are free Internet-based tools that require no download, such as WeVideo, that can be used for editing your videos online.

LABOR ORGANIZATIONS & ALLIANCES

Labor organizations are powerful, well funded, and influential in political campaigns. Their support, whether through financial donation or votes, can make or break a political campaign. Labor organizations, being that they are unions, are created for the purpose of collective bargaining and empowering the rights of its members. It is important to be pro-active in make contacts with union leaders, hearing their concerns, and answering their questions. Each labor union has a political director, government affairs director, or business manager that is responsible for political action. By creating an alliance or receiving an endorsement from a labor union, you increase the chances of being able to raise funds faster than without their endorsement. In addition to raising funds, labor organizations will assist in your campaign by canvassing or knocking on doors, making phone calls from your phone bank or call center, and generally volunteering to help you succeed. Labor organizations have distinct hierarchies which should be respected and in order to advance, it is important to identify the key decision-makers in that organization. Alliances can also be

WHEN THE SLEEPER WAKES!
—*The Passing Show* (London).

made with trade organizations, depending on their political stance. Create a Microsoft Excel spreadsheet that contains the names, addresses, phone numbers, email addresses, general information, and the last thing you spoke about so that you will know where to begin the next time you speak. Before contacting any organization, know the reason you are contacting them and what you seek to gain from the alliance. If you are seeking an endorsement, it is proper to give personal attention to the individual you are seeking the endorsement from. Be wary of any public leaders, officials, and/or community leaders that are willing to trade an endorsement for money. Since you are seeking their endorsement, you should be willing to assist the individual in a mutually beneficial manner so as to not create any negative feelings. If you do not receive an official endorsement from an organization or an individual in an organization, do not be discouraged. The way you behave and act after being denied the endorsement reflects on your character and your public image. Do not harbor feelings of resentment or anger and move forward by contacting other organizations with a similar purpose.

Labor organizations depend on their ability to mobilize their membership for political action that will prevent harmful legislation or support legislation that will assist their goals. They have a "well-oiled political machine" that features automated phone banks for the mass delivery of automated messages, protest signs created and ready for distribution, flyers or handbills that "sell" the views of the organization, trained volunteers that engage in various political task, press contacts that any campaign manager would yearn for, and a highly experienced political action committee (PAC) of a few individuals drawn from its own labor pool. The individuals that comprise this PAC are educated in campaign politics, press management, labor organizing, political advertising, negotiations, and viral political marketing. This is the reason why it is vital for your campaign, whether supporting an organization or candidate, to make the pro-active step in reaching out to labor organizations, association, groups, and stakeholders that can benefit from your issue or stance on issues.

ORGANIZING A RALLY OR PROTEST

Non-violent resistance is a very important movement in that it changed the way people view resistance. Resistance was almost always viewed as violent or conflictive. Mohandas Gandhi, an Indian lawyer, used the Salt Tax as a reason to march 240 miles to the Indian Ocean to protest the British Empire's tax on Indian Ocean salt. As a general rule, for every one hour that is spent on politically advertising the rally or protest, one person will attend. Rallies and protests attract individuals

(A1)

(TO SAVE) HIGHER EDUCATION
(YOU MUST) RALLY

Higher Education Rally!!! November 3, 2009. 14,385 students attend ▓▓▓▓, I need all 14,385 out on Nov. 3rd in support of ▓▓▓ for Higher Education.

They can threaten our programs but we can fight back with our voice in numbers.

The ▓▓▓▓▓▓▓▓▓ and the powers that be are using ▓▓▓▓ as a guinea pig to cut programs left and right. Are you going to allow this? What will it take for you to care? Make signs and gather Rallyers!!! When will you wake up??? Use your Voice! !! Use it!!! Let's together send a message to the ▓▓▓▓▓▓▓, the ▓▓▓▓ Assembly, and the ▓▓▓▓▓.

DO NOT ALLOW ANYONE TO CUT OUR ACADEMIC PROGRAMS!!

BE IN FRONT OF ▓▓▓▓▓ AT ▓▓▓▓ WITH SIGNS AND YOUR VOICE!!!

TUESDAY NOVEMBER 3rd, 2009 at 11:30am-12:30 pm in front of ▓▓▓▓

that are politically active and tend to be avoided by individuals that are suffering from political apathy.

Although you should try to reach out to individuals that do not care about politics, you will be facing an uphill climb because these individuals have chosen to be politically inactive. The first thing that should be created is a flyer **(a1)** for mass distribution when promoting the event. Carry the flyers with you at all times and distribute them to as many people as possible. Place them on top of lunch tables that multiple individuals sit at and be prepared with enough quantities to give them to other organizers that can assist with their distribution. Colleges and universities are great locations for the distribution of such materials, but be sure to only have students attending them, distributing them. Create a Facebook Event, invite all your friends, and ask them to invite all of their friends. Write a press release for the event and send it the relevant reporters or the news desk of the newspaper. If it is a radio show or television station, then contact the producer. Contact local

Higher Education Rally

February 16th, 2010 at 10:30am
In Front of ███████████████

Sponsored by:

community leaders and organizations that have a

stake in supporting the event. Create signs for

advertising the rally or protest, ranging from banner size to 18x24 poster size that can be placed in public areas.

Create handheld signs for your protestors to carry during the event. The handheld signs can be order online, created at home, or in the office. The base that holds the sign is a long, sturdy but flexible wooden stick. The sign itself is a piece of rectangular poster board stuffed with foam on the inside and white cardstock material on the outside. This can be found at most major stationary and home supply retailers.

A sample flyer that was used in an education protest.

The advantage that the foam stuffed poster board has is that it can be cut and shaped to the needs of the user. The stick should be applied along the middle of the foam poster board with wood glue in a cross side fashion. Using a stencil kit and large or wide edged permanent markers, color in the letters to provide a professional look to the signs.

Make a phone bank list spreadsheet in Microsoft Excel in order to call everyone you know that has protested with you, and/or supported your protest. Order the phone bank list based on your most important supporters first to your least important supporters last. Importance is based on the number of times they have supported past events. Create a field in the spreadsheet so that you can create a category for each individual. Assign each individual a type in the category field. Individuals are either organizers, protestors, supporters, and "possibles". Organizers are individuals that have the ability to reach many individuals because of their influence, expert power, or other combinations of factors which give them importance. Protestors are individuals that will attend the protest and rally, wholeheartedly participating in the spirit of the issue for which the event has been organized. Supporters may or may not attend the event, but they will be open to sharing the event on their Facebook profile, emailing their friends, occasionally making phone calls, and helping with the distribution of flyers. "Possibles" or individuals that are un-decisive and have not committed to any action, should not be ignored. Possibles are able to graduate to supporters if the message is delivered enough to stimulate them to action, even if minimal. The key is to not antagonize the possibles so recruiting them will become impossible! Focus on the message and how the issue is affecting them. Emails and phone calls should be placed once again , the night before the event. It is important to speak to the press contacts you have sent press releases to the day before the events in order to synchronize a time to meet the reporter and photographer before the event starts. It is vital to have a megaphone to not have to shout and hurt your throat. A prepared three to five minute speech should be written two to three days prior to the event so as to give you ample to practice the tone, beats, and delivery of the speech. There should be large quantities of water bottles available for the protestors and keep one bottle with you to refresh your voice. If the protestors will be chanting, as most protestors do, you will have to have prepared eight to ten protests chants that will convey the message and the issue the event is representing. The "chant sheet" or printed paper sheet with list of chants should be printed before hands and given to protestors.

CREATING A POLITICAL ACTION COMMITTEE

According to the United States Federal Election Commission, "the term political action committee (PAC) refers to two distinct types of political committees registered with the FEC: separate segregated funds (SSFs) and non-connected committees. Basically, SSFs are political committees established and administered by corporations, labor unions, membership organizations or trade associations. These committees can only solicit contributions from individuals associated with connected or sponsoring organization. By contrast, non-connected committees, as their name suggests, are not sponsored by or connected to any of the aforementioned entities and are free to solicit contributions from the general public."

This means that your campaign you can create a PAC with the purpose of supporting federal, state, and local candidates that are in support of your issue. This gives your organization or issue leverage when dealing with candidates for political office. Candidates that are not in favor of your issue will be more likely to be open to discussion with you when they know your organization has money to donate. That is why an effective PAC is comprised of several members that can donate and pool their resources for the purpose of achieving movement on the issue at hand. PAC's can only make independent expenditures in that they cannot communicate and/or coordinate with the campaign they are supporting. To do otherwise would be illegal, and would create liabilities that can be exploited by the opponents of the campaign you are supporting.

GET OUT THE VOTE (GOTV)

Countless hours spent campaigning and working thousands of hours come down to one day, the day of the vote. In order to win, you must successfully be able to mobilize the voters and even give them rides to the voting booth if needed.

GOTV COMPONENTS

Phone Banking – Volunteers assigned to make phone calls to voters.

Bulk Email – Bulk email sent to thousands of voters to mobilize them to vote for you.

Canvassing – Volunteers assigned to knock on the doors on voters to mobilize them to vote for you.

Exit Pollers – Volunteers assigned by your Campaign organization to inquire from voters how they voted on various issues or political candidates.

SAMPLE GOTV EMAIL
Today is Election Day!
Make time to vote today, Tuesday, June 5th, 2016

Polls are open until 8 p.m.

You vote here:

(NAME OF VOTING PLACE)

(ADDRESS OF VOTING PLACE)

Please remember that **you or your relative can drop off your mail-in ballot** at any polling place in (Name of Location) today.

Even if you've lost your ballot, you can still vote today. Just go to the polling place above and ask for a Provisional Ballot. Poll workers will be happy to help you.

Hope to see you at the polls today.

YOUR NAME

YOUR WEBSITE

POLITICAL REPORT CARD – YOU FLUNK!

Politicians can be gauged according to their platform message and the follow through in which they vote on important regulations and laws. For example, if a certain politician is claiming to be in favor of protecting the rights of immigrants and politically advertises this matter, then votes against a law that would protect the rights of immigrants, this should be recorded and registered by you, and publicly expressed so that the politician realizes that they will be held accountable. The sole purpose of the political report card is to hold politicians accountable and to politically advertise the political report card so that the public should become aware.

POLITICAL REPORT CARD

CANDIDATES NAME	DATE	GRADE
SUPPORTED FUNDING FOR EDUCATION		
REDUCED POLLUTION (AIR, STREET, ETC.)		
PUBLIC SERVICES(UTILITIES, STREET MAINTENANCE, ETC.)		
CREATED EMPLOYMENT OPPORTUNITIES OR JOBS		
REVITALIZED ABANDONED AREAS IN DELAPIDATION		
REDUCED CRIME		
SUPPORTED SOCIAL EQUALITY(GAY MARRIAGE, MINORITY RIGHTS, ETC.)		
REDUCED COST OF LIVING		
INCREASED QUALITY OF HEALTH CARE		
INCREASED ACCESS TO HEALTH CARE		
BALANCED THE BUDGET(LOCAL, STATE, FEDERAL, ETC.)		
REDUCED DEPENDENCE ON LOANS		
SUPPORTED LABOR UNIONS		
ATTRACTED NEW BUSINESSES TO AREA		
CREATED A BUSINESS FRIENDLY ENVIRONMENT		
INVESTED IN CRIME PREVENTION PROGRAMS(GANG INTERVENTION, ETC.)		

GLOSSARY

A

Ad Impression– Website page view.

Agent Provocateur – Political agent that instigates, incites, and/or causes others to engage in political action.

Agitprop– Art that is created for the purpose of conveying a political message. It is a combination of the words agitation and propaganda.

Art Director – Individual responsible for managing the creation or visualization of advertisements.

Astroturfing – Creating a grassroots-like movement that is in fact backed by corporations.

Attack Ad – Advertisement created with the purpose of creating negative public opinion about an issue, organization, or individual.

B

Bandwaggoning– Following whatever cause, candidate, or issue that is more popular without using analysis or contemplation to determine the benefits and costs.

Bleed – Text or image that extends outside the margin to the end of the page.

Body Man – Personal assistant to a political candidate. Takes care of personal chores related to candidate, rather than campaign activities.

Blamestorming – What many campaigns do after a loss instead of drawing lessons from the defeat.

Brainstorming – Process for thinking of new ideas, where individuals give input without their being a correct or incorrect idea, although a moderator may intervene to keep the process uniform.

Branding Continuity – The process of making all campaign materials feature an identical message, identical colors, identical fonts, identical designs, and identical imagery.

Branding – The process of creating awareness and capturing mindshare.

C

Canvassing – Visiting homes and offices with the purpose of collecting donations, signatures, and or support from the home or business owner. Also known as knocking on doors.

Coattails – Using the popularity of one politician in order to benefit another politician.

Comparative Political Advertising – A side by side comparison of two political candidates or the pro's and con's of an issue, printed in an ad form.

Conversion Rate – The percentage of people that take an action (vote for you, support you, endorse you, etc.) from viewing your advertisement. If 1,000 people see your billboard and 100 of them vote for you or donate to your campaign, then your conversion rate %10.

Copywriters – Individuals that write the words used in advertising.

Cost per vote (CPV) – The dollar amount spent per person to earn their vote.

CPM – Cost per thousand. The cost for every one thousand times an advertisement is shown. Used when calculating political advertising return on investment(PAROI).

D

Dark horse – Candidate or bill that is highly unlikely to win or advance, but does so surprisingly.

Deceptive Advertising – Advertisement that deceives or misleads.

De-marketing – Process of reducing demand and support for your organization, issue, or candidate.

Demographics – Age, education level, marital status,

etc. *See Segmentation.*

Direct Mail – Mass mailings sent with the purpose of creating awareness, marketing an event, or soliciting donations.

E

Election – Procedure by which voter choose from among several candidates to hold public office.

Endorsement – Official support or backing from an individual or organization.

F

Fairness Doctrine – Policy enacted by the Federal Communication Commission that broadcasters present both sides of an issue.

Federal Communication Commission – Independent agency responsible for overseeing all radio, television, newspaper, print, and internet communication.

Federal Election Commission – Independent

agency responsible for overseeing all federal elections in the United States including that of the POTUS, Senate, and House of Representatives.

Flip-flop – Taking two sides on the same issue.

Flanking political marketing attack – Choosing a political position that is not addressed by your opponent(s).

Frontloading – Spending the majority of advertising dollars during the start of a political campaign.

G

Graft – The misuse of public office for personal financial gain or benefit.

Grandstanding – Acting in a manner, usually during a speech or an interview, that would project a favorable image for the audience.

H

Handbill – 8.5 x 11 inch flyer.

Hardball – Not giving concessions or not yielding

during political negotiations.

Hatch Act – Federal law that prohibits federal employees, excluding the POTUS and the VPOTUS, from engaging in political activities.

Horse Trading – Giving a concession to an individual or group with the promise or delivery of a similar benefit or concession.

I

Indoctrination – Instilling a dogmatic system of thoughts and beliefs while rejecting open debate and discussion.

In-flight Advertising – Print magazine and closed circuit television advertising targeted to individuals in an airplane.

Insertion Order – Purchase order issued by the media buyer to an advertising salesperson.

Interest Group – Organization created to lobby the government on behalf of its membership.

J

Junket – Negative term used to denote a trip of public officials at the public expense.

K

Key Art – Main image or picture that is used in all the political advertising materials of a campaign.

Kingmaker – An individual that is very influential and is able to influence the selection of public officials.

L

L.U.R. – Lowest Unit Rate. The lowest possible price a television ad space salesperson can offer you. Also known as Lowest Unit Charge.

M

Matte – Not reflective of light. Opposite of glossy.

Media Buyer – Individual responsible for purchasing media space, airtime, and television spots for the placement of advertisements.

Media Planner – Individual responsible for planning the annual media buying calendar.

Meminism – Movement of males that support equal pay in the workplace for women.

Mindshare – Creation of recent awareness in the mind of the consumer, supporter, or voter when thinking of your brand, organization, or candidate.

N

Non-Zero Sum Game – Cooperating rather than competing to gain. There can be more than one winner in a non-zero sum game.

O

Ombudsman – Official governmental employee assigned to solve problems between elected officials and constituents by assisting constituents with their needs.

Opposition Research – Program within the campaign that analyzes the strengths, weaknesses, movements, and actions of competitors. Also known as Competitive Intelligence or Business Intelligence.

P

Political Machine – A political campaign that has its infrastructure and processes prepared and has been tested in previous campaigns.

Positioning – Differentiating your message by selecting issues that are not being used by other candidates or organizations.

POTUS – President of the United States.

Press Release – Advertisement written in the form of a news article in order to promote "newsworthiness" but has the real goal of shaping public opinion in regards to an issue, organization, or individual.

Primetime – Television between 6pm to 12am midnight. The most expensive time to run a commercial because it is the time with the most viewers.

R

Rate Card – Price sheet for advertising in radio, television, newspaper, magazine, and other media publications.

Rational Appeal – Use of logic and reason in advertisements instead of the appeal to emotion.

Realpolitik – Policy based on practical politics rather than ideology.

S

Segmentation – Dividing potential supporters or voters by voter frequency, age, education, lifestyle, etc.

Swiftboating – Negative attacks used during campaigns, that have no basis in truth.

Spot – 15 second to 60 second commercial on television. Also media space.

Social Labeling – Creation of categories for social classes.

Spot Rate – Cost per television spot.

Stump – To campaign.

Subtext – Hidden meaning.

T

Teaser – 15 to 30 second commercial.

U

Under-handed – Term that denotes secret and unfair political dealings.

V

Viral Marketing – Word of mouth marketing.

VPOTUS – Vice President of the United States.

W

Warranty – A promise that the service or product you are providing is indeed the same one that was advertised.

Wheeler-Lea Act – Federal law enacted in 1938, that prohibits false or mis-leading advertising.

NOTE

This glossary does not contain **every** term that is used in politics and advertising, as there are **tens of thousands** of terms used, that this book will not be able to list. The terms that are however listed and used above are general enough so as to be used by most individuals working in political advertising.

POLITICAL ART

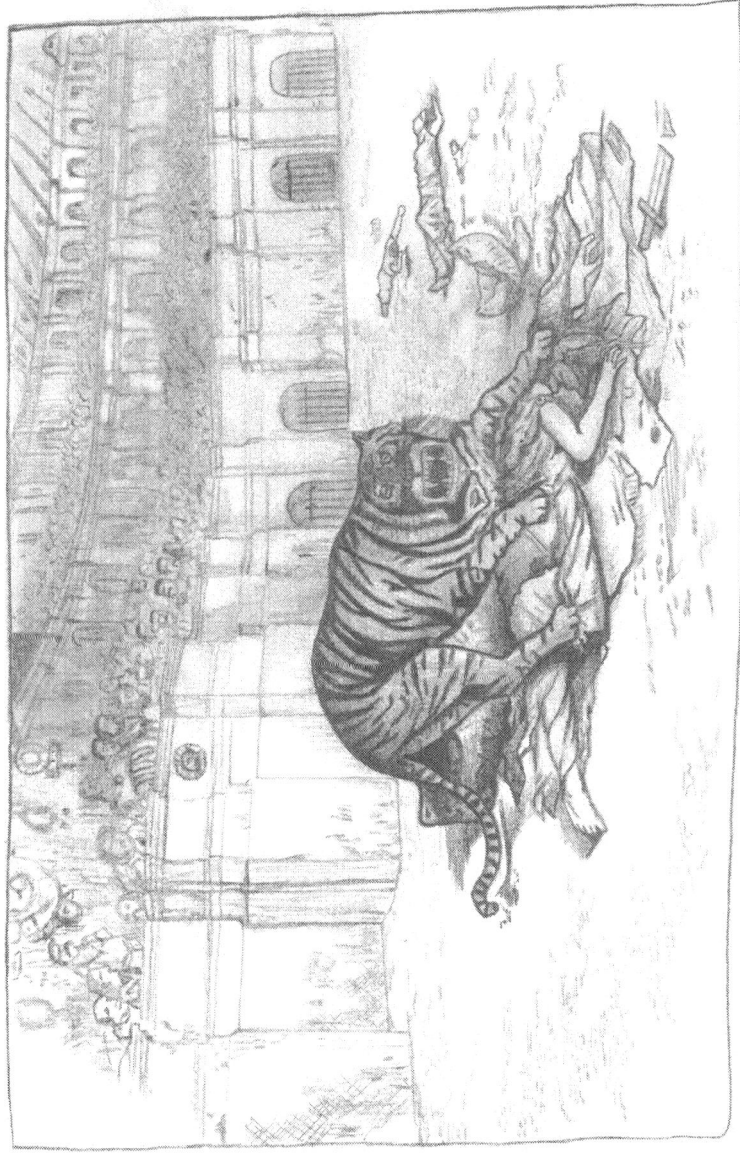

WHY POLITICS IS VITAL

Politics is the process in which resources are allocated, to whom they are allocated, and how much to each body is allocated. If you do not participate in politics, you have no say in what you receive. It is more likely than not, the local politician or the local political issue that can affect your quality of living. It is for this reason that this manual was written, to empower individuals by equipping them with the necessary tools to influence the political agenda. This book is in no way the end all or the final word on political campaigning, but rather, it is an understandable guide to be followed loosely and adapted to the political situation you are confronted with. I hope that it helps you achieve your goals.

Sincerely,

Kambiz Mostofizadeh
Author
Political Advertising Manual

BIBLIOGRAPHY

(1) McNamara, Michael. 2008. "The Political Campaign Desk Reference". Pg .128. Outskirts Press, Inc. Denver, CO

(2) Thomas Robert J. 1999. "How to Run for Local Office". Pg. 47. R& T Enterprise Inc. Westland, MI

(3) Diamond, Edwin and Bates, Stephen. 1988. "The Spot: The Rise of Political Advertising on Television". Pg. 42, 45, 46. 78, 66, 49, 93, 105, 115, 116, 120, 169, 170, 244, 247. Cambridge, MA

Political Advertising Manual
(Please use this page for notes and comments)

Political Advertising Manual
(Please use this page for notes and comments)

Political Advertising Manual
(Please use this page for notes and comments)

Political Advertising Manual
(Please use this page for notes and comments)

Political Advertising Manual
(Please use this page for notes and comments)

Political Advertising Manual
(Please use this page for notes and comments)

Political Advertising Manual
(Please use this page for notes and comments)

Political Advertising Manual
(Please use this page for notes and comments)

Political Advertising Manual
(Please use this page for notes and comments)

Acknowledgments

Dr. Annie Wilson Whetmore,

Mikazuki Publishing House,

Hoornaz Mostofizadeh,

Dr. Jay Kaplan,

Shahla Mostofizadeh,

Nasser Mostofizadeh,

American Political Science Association,

American Association of Political Consultants,

Dr. Caroline Bordinaro,

Dr. Hamoud Salhi,

California State University system,

My brothers Ali & Bobby

All individuals that strive for perfection

MIKAZUKI PUBLISHING HOUSE TITLES

Mikazuki Jujitsu Manual

ISBN-10: 0615473113 (Print)

ISBN-13: 9780615473116 (Print)

ISBN-10: 0615480543 (E-Book)

Author: Kambiz Mostofizadeh

Genre: Sports/Non-Fiction

Pages: 125 (Print)

Release Date: May 2011

Print Retail Price: $24.99

E-book Retail Price: $14.99

Description: Jujitsu was the battlefield art of the Samurai who used the techniques to defend themselves when they had lost their weapon and were facing an armed opponent. But in today's environment where random violence is a certainty, the knowledge of jujitsu has empowered countless individuals with the art of the samurai for self defense.

The book by Kambiz Mostofizadeh is a jujitsu manual explaining core jujitsu techniques, shares the principles and applications of ju or yielding, covers Jujitsu's Japanese origins, teaches methods for fighting against multiple attackers, includes techniques for defeating mixed martial artists, and divulges strategies for offensive and defensive maneuvers. The book features more than 20 hand drawn illustrations representing the various techniques used within jujitsu. Mikazuki Jujitsu Manual; Learn Jujitsu also features a glossary of jujitsu terms, annual jujitsu tournaments, and methods for defeating a boxer. The author said "I wrote this book as a guide for my students and any student of modern martial arts. I believe all people can benefit from the study of martial arts, because the need for personal safety and protection is essential to everyone".

Karate 360

ISBN-10: 0983594627 (Print)

ISBN-13: 9780983594628 (Print)

ISBN-13: 978-0-9835946-7-3 (E-book)

Author: Kambiz Mostofizadeh

Genre: Sports/Non-Fiction

Print Retail Price: $14.99

E-book Retail Price: $4.99

Pages: 115 (Print)

Release Date: December 2011

Description: Explore Karate's roots, learn key karate techniques, and learn why Karate is the world's most popular martial art.

EXCERPT - "The essence of Karate is defense. The powerful leg strikes, efficient blocking techniques, and strong punches evolved in to an effective martial art that eventually became the most popular martial art in the world".

25 Principles of Martial Arts

ISBN-13: 9780983594604 (Print)

ISBN-10: 0983594619 (E-Book)

Author: Kambiz Mostofizadeh

Genre: Philosophy/Non-Fiction

Pages: 111 (Print)

Release Date: November 2011

Print Retail Price: $14.99

E-book Retail Price: $7.99

EXCERPT - "Large amount of resources and more individuals in your organization do not necessarily equate to victory over your opponent if you have lost the advantage of formlessness."

Description: Learn the 25 key principles of martial arts and the strategies that make them successful. This book divulges strategies and tactics that can be applied in the dojo, in your personal life, and in your business affairs.

Letting the Customers Win

ISBN-10: 0983594651 (Print)

ISBN-13: 9780983594659 (Print)

ISBN-13: 978-0-9835946-8-0 (E-book)

Author: Kambiz Mostofizadeh

Genre: Business/Non-Fiction

Pages: 120

Release Date: February 2011

Print Retail Price: $14.99

E-book Retail Price: $9.99

Description: Millions of dollars are spent to attract customers, while little is spent to keep current customers happy. It is 7 more times expensive to gain new business than it is to keep your current customer. This book reveals customer care strategies including call center management, customer loyalty card schemes, and relationship marketing.

Find the Ideal Husband

ISBN-10: 0983594694 (E-book)

ISBN-13: 9780983594697 (E-book)

Author: Kambiz Mostofizadeh

Genre: Self-help/Non-Fiction

Pages: 110 (E-book)

Release Date: Valentine's Day 2012

E-book Retail Price: $9.99

Description: The ideal husband is rich, classy, happy, handsome, and caring. Learn where to meet the ideal husband and how to recognize the indicators for knowing he is the right choice. Let the search begin!

Learning Magic

ISBN-10: 0983594635 (Print)

ISBN-13: 978-0983594635 (Print)

Author: Kambiz Mostofizadeh

Genre: Performing Arts/Non-Fiction

Pages: 111 (Print)

Release Date: March 2012

Print Retail Price: $14.99

Description: Learn the fundamentals of performing magic including the reasons why magic tricks are so effective. Whether at home, in the office, or at a gathering, this book will teach you key magic tricks for performing.

Political Advertising Manual

ISBN-10: 0983594643 (Print)

ISBN-13: 9780983594642 (Print)

ISBN-13: 978-0-9835946-8-0 (E-book)

Author: Kambiz Mostofizadeh

Genre: Political Science/Non-Fiction

Pages: 119 (Print)

Release Date: Jan 2012

Print Retail Price: $14.99

E-book Retail Price: $9.99

Description: Political marketing strategies are used by nearly every victorious candidate to achieve electoral victory. Explore key political marketing techniques & tactics for effective message delivery.

Street Food War

ISBN-13: 9781937981006 (Print)

ISBN-13: 978-1-937981-98-3 (E-book)

Author: Kambiz Mostofizadeh

Genre: Food & Culinary Arts/Non-Fiction

Pages: 125 (Print)

Release Date: February 2012

Print Retail Price: $12.99

E-book Retail Price: $7.99

Description: There are millions of food trucks, food carts, and food stalls in the U.S. The fantastic growth of street food and its popularity in television shows, has drawn the interest of millions to the benefits of quality street food. Go behind the scenes of the street food industry and learn how it operates. This is the must-have guide for anyone that loves street food or works in the street food industry.

Living the Pirate Code

ISBN-13: 9781937981013 (Print)

ISBN-13: 9781937981020 (E-book)

Author: Eric Hurtado

Genre: History/Non-Fiction

Pages: 200 (Print)

Release Date: March 2012

Print Retail Price: $19.99

E-book Retail Price: $9.99

Description: Pirates were famous sailors who hunted for gold and treasure. Learn the famous code practiced by pirates and how this impacted their lives. Discover the greatest pirates and how they shaped our modern history.

More Titles Coming Soon
Visit www.MikazukiPublishingHouse.com for more information on our books.

MIKAZUKI PUBLISHING HOUSE - BOOK ORDER FORM – PRINT

(SCAN AND EMAIL TO CUSTOMERCARE@MIKAZUKIPUBLISHINGHOUSE.COM)

BOOK NAME	UNITS	PRICE PER BOOK	SUB-TOTAL
Mikazuki Jujitsu Manual		$9.99	
25 Principles of Martial Arts		$9.99	
Karate 360		$9.99	
Learning Magic		$9.99	
Letting the Customers Win		$9.99	
Political Advertising Manual		$9.99	
Street Food War		$9.99	
Living the Pirate Code		$9.99	
TOTAL		$_____._____ United States Dollars	

Name_____

Address_____

City _____ State/Province_____

Postal Code_____ Country_____

Email Address:_____

Would you like to receive updates in the future about new books, discounts, and information on Mikazuki Publishing House titles?
( ) **Yes**   ( ) **No**

HOW IT WORKS
1. Scan and email this form to:
   customercare@mikazukipublishinghouse.com
2. You will receive an invoice on PayPal. Shipping Costs will be included in invoice. Pay the Invoice.
3. Books will be shipped within 3-4 days of receiving your payment.

Mikazuki Publishing House is a book publishing company specializing in a variety of non-fiction works.

Press Contacts interested in arranging press interviews and/or author appearances, are welcome to contact:

pr@MikazukiPublishingHouse.com

We believe that the written word is the most effective vehicle for the delivery of knowledge and that reading is essential to educating oneself. Mikazuki Publishing House believes in the promotion of reading as a tool for self progression and therefore invests resources, working with libraries and institutions of higher learning, to propagate the advantages of reading. Mikazuki Publishing House also offers free book donations and free book signings/appearances to libraries upon request and upon availability. Mikazuki Publishing House is honored to be an active participant in the fight to reverse world deforestation. Approximately 30 million trees are cut down in the U.S. every year to be used for the creation of print books. We wish to offset and counterbalance the use of paper in the book publishing industry by working with organizations dedicated to reversing the trend of world deforestation. We will first start with one tree. The consequences of not doing so could be disastrous for future generations.

Every minute, over 160 acres of land feel the destructive effects of deforestation. Deforestation causes species to become extinct, disrupts natural habitats, and erodes the top soil of viable farming lands causing drought and famine.

As a responsible book publisher, Mikazuki Publishing House will donate a percentage from the sale of each book to the effort of planting millions of trees.

Mikazuki Publishing House is pleased to invite foundations, associations, and groups dedicated to planting trees to contact us.

Please send all requests to:

philanthropy@MikazukiPublishingHouse.com

Mikazuki Publishing House enables greater exchange of knowledge by providing our authors to public institutions as guest speakers.

As our authors have limited time due to writing and book tours, we ask that you submit a request outlining the type of event with its pertinent information included.

We invite requests from the following types of organizations:

Public Libraries/Book Fairs

Event Management organizations

Community Centers

Community Colleges/Universities

Book Clubs with over 50 Active members

Please send all requests to:
philanthropy@MikazukiPublishingHouse.com

Mikazuki Publishing House is a proud member of the Independent Book Publishers Association

"EDUCATION IS THE KEY TO HAPPINESS"
KAMBIZ MOSTOFIZADEH